The Sunny day Book

Jane Bull

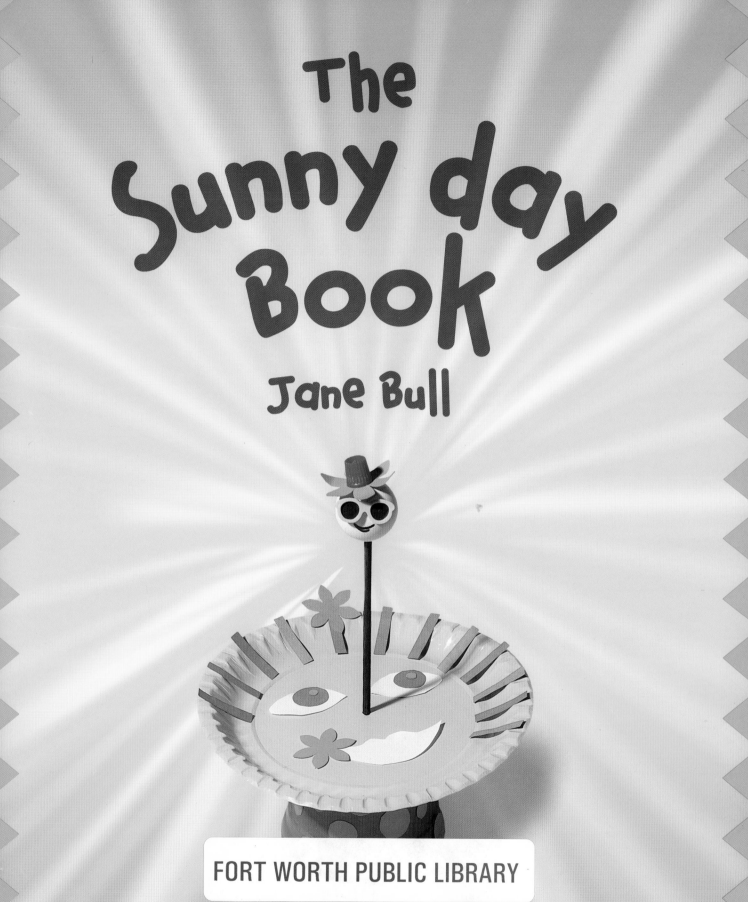

DK Publishing

LONDON, NEW YORK, MUNICH,
MELBOURNE, AND DELHI

DESIGN • Jane Bull
EDITOR • Penelope Arlon
PHOTOGRAPHY • Andy Crawford
DESIGN ASSISTANCE • Sadie Thomas

PUBLISHING MANAGER • Sue Leonard
MANAGING ART EDITOR • Clare Shedden
PRODUCTION • Shivani Pandey
DTP DESIGNER • Almudena Díaz

For Charlotte, Billy, and James

First American Edition, 2004

Published in the United States by
DK Publishing, Inc.
375 Hudson Street
New York, New York 10014

05 06 07 08 10 9 8 7 6 5 4 3 2

A Cataloging-in-Publication record for this book
is available from the Library of Congress.

ISBN: 0-7566-0308-0

Color reproduction by
GRB Editrice S.r.l., Verona, Italy
Printed and bound in China by Toppan.

Discover more at
www.dk.com

keep your cool
in the sunshine

In this Sunny book you'll find...

hundreds of reasons...

to get outdoors!

Sunny time

Track the sun as it moves across the sky, and keep track of time.

Is it time for a drink?

8

9

10

11

noon
12

1

2

Sundials

As the sun moves across the sky, believe it or not, it can tell you the time. Stand something tall, such as a stick in a bucket of sand, in an area that gets sun all day. Each hour, place a shell where the shadow of the stick falls and note what time it is. The next day, you can tell the time by using it!

7

6

5

4

3

4

Fun times in the sun

All you need is a bright sunny day and some things to mark the hours as they pass. If you are on a beach, use shells. Or turn the page to learn how to make a sundial for your backyard.

Check your clock time after time

noon

11 12 1

10 2

9 3

8 4

7 5

6

Make a clock wherever you are.

Making time

Try putting the shells on the tip of the stick shadow and at the end of the day see what shape you have made. It may not be quite circular like a watch. That's weird! If you make the sundial out of pebbles or shells, then you can leave it out all year. Does it work at all times of the sun?

5

Sun clock

Time to watch the clock in the yard.

what time is it?

Impress your friends by being able to tell the time without looking at a watch. How do you do it? By using the sun.

How to make a clock

You will need:

- Paper plate
- Terracotta plant pot
- Stick or garden cane
- Watch
- Strips of paper
- Sticky tack

Before you assemble your sun clock, decorate the plate, stick, and pot.

1. Make a hole in the center of the plate and push the cane through.

Put sticky tack around the hole.

2. Now put the cane through the hole in the plant pot.

Press the plate onto the sticky tack.

3. Make sure the plate doesn't turn easily on the stick.

Use the sunlight to set your clock

You will need a whole sunny day to set your clock so that you can read it the next day.

1. Place your clock in a sunny area.

2. The stick will cast a shadow across the plate. This is the sun telling you the time.

3. Now look at your watch, and mark the shadow on each hour with a strip of paper. For example, at 10 o'clock mark the shadow, then continue until the sun goes down.

4. The next day, tell the time by seeing where the shadow falls!

10 o'clock   12 o'clock   2 o'clock

Noon 12

11 10 9 8

1 2 3 4 5 6 7

It's just past 3 o'clock

Make the 12 o'clock strip look different to remind you where it is.

Take cover

Stay out of the Sun in a homemade hideaway.

Keep the enemy away!

No entry unless you know the password

keep out

Beware!

When the sun is getting too hot and you need some shade, don't go indoors—build a tent in the backyard with some blankets and garden canes.

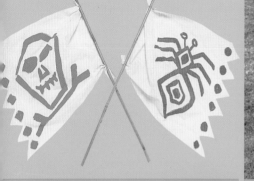

Picnic pots

Setting up camp

Once you've made your camp, you will need food supplies as well as clear notices, such as flags or a sign, to make sure that visitors are unwelcome unless invited. Create a password for your friends.

Setting up camp

The whole idea of a camp is to put it somewhere where you won't be disturbed, and bring plenty of rations with you to keep you going. The beauty of this tent is that you can fold it up, store it, and use it again and again.

For the camp you will need
- 12 bamboo canes
- Strong tape and scissors
- An old blanket or rug
- Clothespins

Tape the sticks together

Lay out the bamboo canes in position as shown and tape each corner and the center securely.

5 ft (1.5 m)

4 ft (1.2 m)

6 ft (1.8 m)

6 ft (1.8 m)

4 ft (1.2 m)

5 ft (1.5 m)

You will need two of these frames for the hideout.

Wrap the tape around and around to make sure it is secure.

Complete your hideaway

Make 2 of these

You will need a friend to help you hold them up.

Stand the two frames up in a triangle shape and tape the two top ends together tightly.

Make sure you make the hideout wide enough to fit inside.

BAMBOO CANES

4 canes at
4 ft (1.2 m)

4 canes at
5 ft (1.5 m)

4 canes at
6 ft
(1.8 m)

Bamboo canes

You will need 12 bamboo canes to make your hideout. If you need to cut them, ask an adult to help you.

Fly the flag

- 1 bamboo cane
- A piece of scrap material
- String

Paint a design on your flag and snip down the edges to make a zigzag pattern. Then bunch up two corners and tie them to the pole with string.

Picnic bowl

- 3 bamboo canes 2 ft (60 cm)
- Strong tape, plastic bowl

Tie the three poles together in the center, let them go, and pop a plastic bowl on top. Fill with rations.

Tie the poles tightly in the middle.

When you let go of the poles, they should fall into a stool shape and balance perfectly on three legs.

Drape the rug or blanket over the top of the framework.

Password, please!

Make a cardboard "do not enter" sign.

Use clothespins to attach the rug to the frame at the bottom.

11

Picnic in a pot
Look, no leftovers!

Edible pots

Anything delicious can be
put into an ice-cream
cone—sweet or salty
snacks. Perfect for
picnics—no mess to
clear up!

popcorn

Surprise pots

Spoon delicious dips into the bottom of your pots and put fruit or vegetables on top.

cream-cheese dip

yogurt or cream

Hummus, guacamole

Mayonnaise

Cover up!

Wear your art on your clothes, and keep the sun off, too!

GraffiT-shirt

Make your mark

Fabric pens are the easiest way to decorate a T-shirt. Draw your design right on, then iron it to make it permanent.

Remember to put paper or cardboard inside the T-shirt to stop the ink from going through.

You will need:
- White or light-colored cotton T-shirt
- Fabric pens

I'm looking at you!

T-shirts

White and pale-colored T-shirts work best when decorating or dying. If you use a dark T-shirt, the decoration won't show as clearly. So get out your old T-shirts and cover up!

Hey! look at me I look good like that

Pack up all your stuff in me!

Transform your clothes

Crazy faces

You could use any material to decorate your hats and bags, but felt is a great fabric to use—it is easy to cut and can be stuck onto other material with white glue or fabric glue.

Practice your face shapes on newspaper first. Then cut them out.

Cut out the shapes.

Use the paper templates to draw on the fabric.

what to do
• Practice your shapes on a piece of newspaper.
• Use your newspaper template to cut out the felt shapes.
• Glue them into position.

Glue the shapes.

white glue

Stick in position.

You will need:
• Scraps of fabric, such as felt
• Newspaper
• Scissors
• PVA or white glue

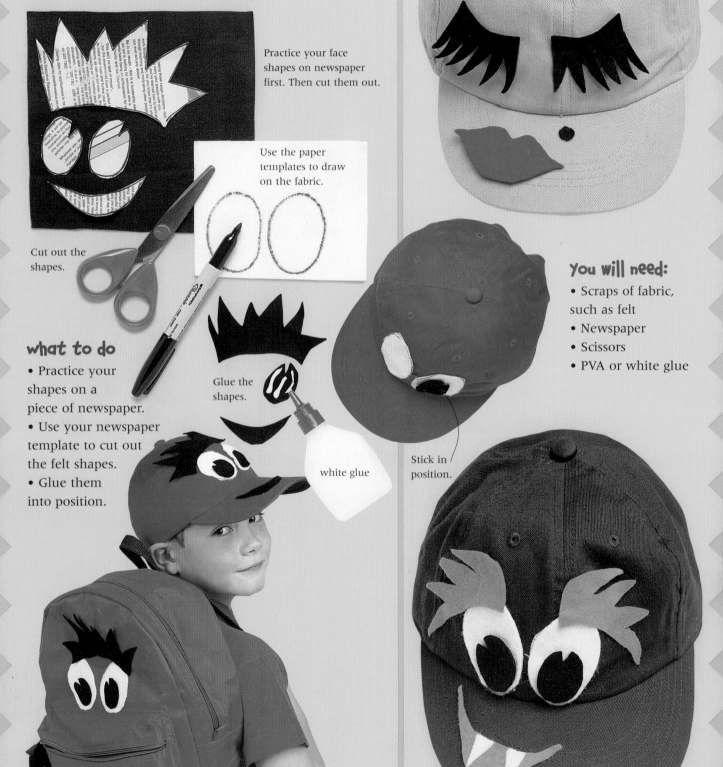

16

Tie-dye T-shirts

The secret to tie-dye is the elastic bands. If they are tied tightly, the dye will not color the tied parts, leaving swirls of pattern. When you are dying fabrics, make sure you read and follow the instructions on the dye package.

⭐ **Ask an adult** to help with hot water.

☀ Tie the bands

Scrunch up pieces of your T-shirt and tie elastic bands tightly to each little scrunch.

Follow the guidelines on the package.

Mix up the dye

Now dunk your T-shirt into the dye and leave for however long the instructions tell you. Use rubber gloves.

Dunk in a T-shirt

Take it out and rinse it

Remember to use a light T-shirt; otherwise, the dye won't show.

Remove the bands

Rinse the T-shirt until the colour stops running out. Remove the elastic bands to reveal the twisty, swirly pattern. Then hang it up in the sun to dry.

The more elastic bands you use, the more patterns you get.

Thirst aid

Instant lemon soothies

to be taken in emergencies.

Lemon remedy contains:

3 MEDIUM LEMONS + 1 QUART (LITER) WATER + SUGAR =

Now sit back and take it squeezy!

Fizzy lemonade

For extra fizz, dilute your lemonade with carbonated mineral water.

Lemon popsicles

Lemon twister

A sugary candy twist with a lemon slice in the middle makes a perfect swizzle stick.

Lemon to go

Wash out empty soda bottles and fill them up with a batch of homemade lemonade.

Crusty, sugary rim

Long cool lemon

Fill a tall glass with lots of ice and let it melt away into your lemonade.

Ice cube lemon pops

ways to add sweetness

• Use candy canes and lollipops as swizzle sticks.
• For a yummy, sugary crust on the rim of the glass, pour some sugar onto a plate. Hold a glass upside down and dip the rim into water, then into the sugar. Leave it to dry.

19

Thirst aid kit

This lemonade recipe will make just over a quart (liter). It may be tangy, so add sugar or extra water until it tastes good. The best thing to do is experiment.

Remember to save some to make ice pops and ice cubes.

Drink up

Your lemonade will only keep for two days in the refrigerator, so drink it quickly!

Squeeze to meet you

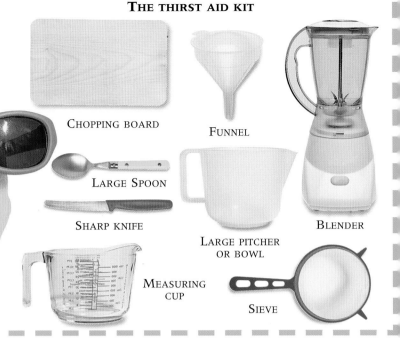

THE THIRST AID KIT

CHOPPING BOARD

FUNNEL

LARGE SPOON

SHARP KNIFE

BLENDER

LARGE PITCHER OR BOWL

MEASURING CUP

SIEVE

Making lemonade

Scrub all the lemons well, since you will use the whole fruit—even the peel!

- 3 lemons
- 1 quart (liter) water
- Sugar to taste

Ask an adult to help with the blender.

1 Wash the lemons and chop each into eight pieces.

2 Put the lemons into a blender and add some of the water.

3 Blend until the mixture is smooth.

Ice cube lemonpops

Place some fruit suckers into an ice-cube tray and fill up with your lemonade. Put them into the freezer overnight and you have ice-cold, fruity lemonade lollipops!

sugar and water

It's best to keep your lemonade in a bottle in the refrigerator.

Gently pour through a funnel.

Hold on tight to the bottle.

4 Pour the mixture into a sieve.

5 Help the juice drain through by pressing it with the back of a spoon.

6 Add some sugar to your taste, and the remaining water.

7 Bottle your lemonade.

Bowls of ice

Bowls of ice that keep things chilled in the hot sun

Ice bowl tips

• To remove your ice bowl, leave it out at room temperature for a while to loosen it.

• Put the ice bowl back in the freezer for a few minutes to cool it again.

• Remember the bowl will melt in the hot sun, so eat up!

Freeze an ice bowl

Keep your food and drinks cool in a chilly ice bowl. You could use other fruit around the edges, or even flowers and leaves.

1. Place a smaller bowl inside a larger one. Cut two lemons into thin slices and position them in the gap between the bowls.

2. Fill the gap with water. Place a stone in the center of the small bowl and tape it securely to the larger bowl to hold it in place.

3. Put it in the freezer overnight. When you take it out, run cold water over it to loosen the bowls. Gently remove the bowls to reveal your ice bowl!

Fill your bowl with fruit. Quick—eat it up before it melts!

Don't lose your cool

The BIG freeze
Hello, ice to meet you!

Keep ultra-cool on a hot, sunny day.
Create icy shapes and turn them ice blue.

Blue cubes

For blue ice cubes, add food coloring to the water before you fill up the tray.

Sugar-coated cooler

Dip the top rim of a glass in some water.

Now dip the rim in a dish of sugar.

The sugar will stick to the glass.

Fill with lemonade and drop in the ice cubes. Look how it turns blue—how refreshing!

Ice sculpture cocktail

Not just cubes—water will freeze into any shape you like. Try a balloon, the bottom of a plastic bottle, or even a rubber glove for some really spooky frozen fingers!

Add food coloring to the water before you freeze it to make colored ice

Ice tips

• For hand and balloon shapes, make sure you keep the water in by tying up the balloon or using a clothespin on the rubber glove. You may have to cut the balloon and the glove to release them, so make sure you use an old glove.

• Run the shapes under cold water if they are difficult to take out of their molds.

Rubber glove

Frozen fingers

Balloon

Rain cloud

Jell-O mold

Snowball

Floating flower

Plastic bottle base

Iceberg

Plastic bag

watch out! Shark attack!

Grrrrrrr

Let's move it!

Go, go, go!

keep your cool

What floats and what doesn't? It's a matter of life and death if there are vicious sharks in the water. Quick, get this boat out of here!

Crafty boats

Think or you'll sink! All you need to remember is, if it floats it'll make a boat. You'll need it to float if the sharks are around!

use anything you can find that floats for boat-building materials

To make a basic boat

All you need are two plastic bottles and a plastic food tray. When you are finished, add special features, such as a control deck or a racing spoiler.

Carefully make a hole in each corner.

Plastic bottle   Plastic food tray   Plastic bottle

Scissors and string

Tie a piece of string through each hole and tightly around each bottle.

⭐ **Ask an adult** to help when you are near water.

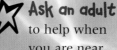

Fluttering flags and bunting to liven up your sunny day party.

Bags of flags

Transform plastic shopping bags into festive banners that flutter in the breeze.

Start collecting
colorful plastic bags

Bags of fun
Every time someone
in your family goes
shopping, keep the plastic
bags. You'll be amazed
how useful they can be!

How to make flags from bags

Bags of bunting

All you have to do is make a template in a triangle shape. Cut the triangles out of plastic bags and attach them with string. Have bags of fun!

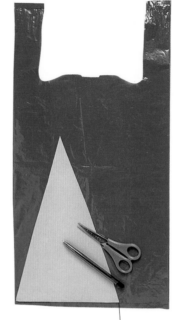

Cut out a paper triangle template.

Draw a line around the paper.

Cut out lots and lots of colorful triangles.

Bags of flags

Cut a plastic soda bottle into bands to make the perfect flag support to tape strips of plastic to. Perfect to hang up in a breezy place to flutter in the wind.

Cut out a colorful piece of plastic bag and stick over the bottle band.

☆ **Ask an adult** to help cut the bottle.

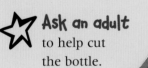

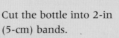

Cut the bottle into 2-in (5-cm) bands.

Cut strips of plastic and tape them to the plastic band.

Lay the triangles in a row and place a long piece of string along the bottom.

Tape the string in place.

Fold the plastic over the string and staple it in place.

Wrap the band into a circular shape and attach the ends with tape.

Attach some string to the band and hang it up outside.

Streamers on parade

You will need:
• A plastic cup • Garden cane • Plastic bag • Scissors • Glue • Tape

Cut out the base of a cup.

Make two holes in the side for the cane.

Use a sharp pencil to make the holes.

Push the cane through the holes.

Glue the cane in place and add modeling clay for decoration.

Bring the folded bag up through the bottom of the cup.

Fold the bag so that it is a strip about 2 in (4 cm) wide.

Bring the bag over the cane and tape it in place.

Add some decoration

Starting from the bottom, cut the bag into strips about 1 in (2 cm) wide to the base of the cup.

Streaming by
By running and running with the streamers in the sunshine, you will make a whooshing sound behind you. When you are finished running, plant them in the ground and let them wave in the breeze.

watch us race with swishing streamers

Party time!

33

Sun catchers

Shimmering, glittering mobiles

twist and turn in the breeze, catching the bright sunlight.

Silver scraps

Look out for things lying around the house that reflect the sun. Try old CDs, gift wrap, and shiny plastic bottles.

How to catch the sun

Jazz up your backyard by finding anything that shines, glitters, or shimmers, and make mobiles with it. As they twist and turn in the sunlight, they glisten and dance. And on a cloudy day, they will still cheer up the yard.

Spiral catcher

The basic shape of this sun-catcher is the spiral of aluminum foil and a used CD. But with a bit of imagination, you can turn it into a real dazzler. Add sequins, shiny buttons, old Christmas decorations, or even double up the spiral and make an enormous spiral catcher!

String

Twisted foil

CD

1. Cut about 2 ft (60 cm) of aluminum foil.

2. Scrunch and twist it up in your hands until it is a solid tube.

3. Twist it around your hand. Add another for a longer spiral.

4. Tie a piece of string to the top of the spiral, then tie the other end around a CD.

Leave some extra string at the top to hang it up.

Decide where you want the CD to hang before you tie it.

Dancing paper plate

The secret to the paper plate catcher is to decorate both sides of the plate—that way, whichever way it turns, it will sparkle.

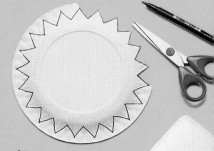

1. Draw a zigzag around a paper plate and cut it out.

Shiny candy wrapper

2. Now cover it with lots of shiny things.

Foil dish

Sequins

3. Tape some string to the back and add any other shiny things you can find.

Christmas ornament

Bottle-bell mobile

• Take some string and attach a round piece of posterboard, 1 in (3 cm) across, halfway along it by poking a hole through the card.
• Thread a button below it.
• Attach shiny decorations such as CDs, ornaments, and anything else that shimmers.
• Now simply thread the bottle-bell through the top of the string and it will sit on the posterboard.

Posterboard

Button

String

CD

Ornament

How to make the bottle-bell

1. Cut off the bottom of a soda bottle.

2. Cut 1/2-in (2 cm-) strips about two-thirds of the way up the bottle.

3. Roll each strip up with your fingers and they will curl.

These old, shiny gift bows are perfect. Squeeze two together and they will stay attached!

Let's sparkle in the sunlight

Thread the bottle-bell along the string until it sits on the posterboard.

4. Thread the string through the neck of the bottle.

Tiny camps for tiny toys

A camp within a camp.
On the ed of your backyard camp sits another tir adventure world. Let's get building!

This way to the building site

Portable campsite

Camps on trays are very useful because you can take them inside if it rains. You could use anything to decorate your landscape—you could even add a little soil and plant some small flowers in it. Work out what you would like best in a campsite and get building!

Twig frame tent

Gather up some small twigs, make the frame, and hang a piece of material over it.

Tie tightly with string.

For the legs, tie three twigs together at the top.

Stand the two ends up an place another twig across them for the tent frame.

Tiny swing

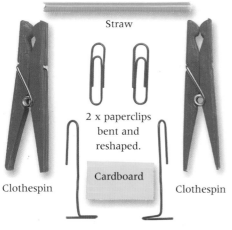

Straw

2 x paperclips bent and reshaped.

Cardboard

Clothespin   Clothespin

Tape the paperclips to the cardboard to make a seat. Then hook them over the straw.

Baby bunting

Find some pieces of colored paper and a long piece of string.

Cut the paper into diamond shapes.

Glue one side of the diamond.

Fold it over the string with the glue on the inside to form a triangle.

Get camping!

Put it together! Take a tray and fill it will sand, gravel, or soil. Find some pebbles or rocks and place them around the edge. Now use your imagination to fill it with teeny, tiny camping gear.

I can't wait to move in

Pebbles create a good landscape.

Use pebbles to keep the material down

A tiny picnic stand made with three twigs and a bottle top.

Sponge fish

A pond made out of a food container.

You could use sand as your base

41

Casting Shadows

View the world from some strange angles using shadows from the sun, and then capture them on camera.

Snap happy! Don't be camera-

You will need:
- A camera—single-use cameras are handy
- Some willing models
- Your imagination
- Lots of bright sunshine

Special effects

Hand shadows against a wall are great, but why not use your whole body to create some really strange shadow effects? You could even make up a story based on your shadow photos.

Fun in the Sun – what can we play?

Make a water bomb

1 Fold a square piece of paper along the dotted lines as shown here.

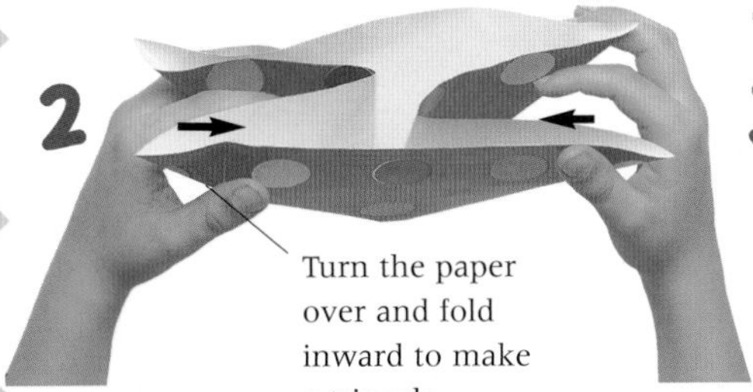

2 Turn the paper over and fold inward to make a triangle.

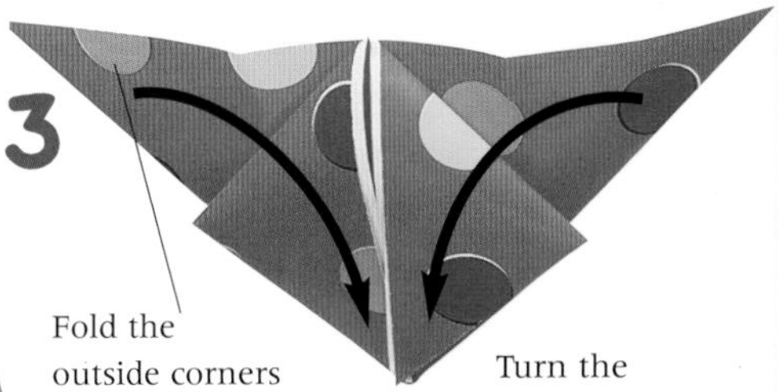

3 Fold the outside corners to meet the central point.

Turn the paper over and repeat.

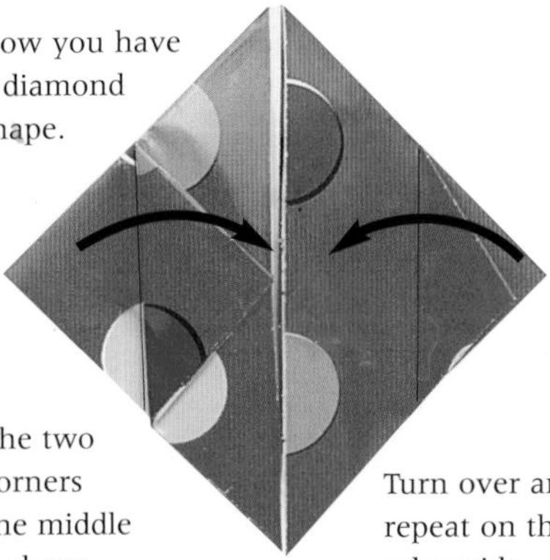

4 Now you have a diamond shape.

Fold the two side corners into the middle of the shape.

Turn over and repeat on the other side.

5 Fold the top corner flaps down and poke into the gaps made by step 4. Turn over and repeat the other side.

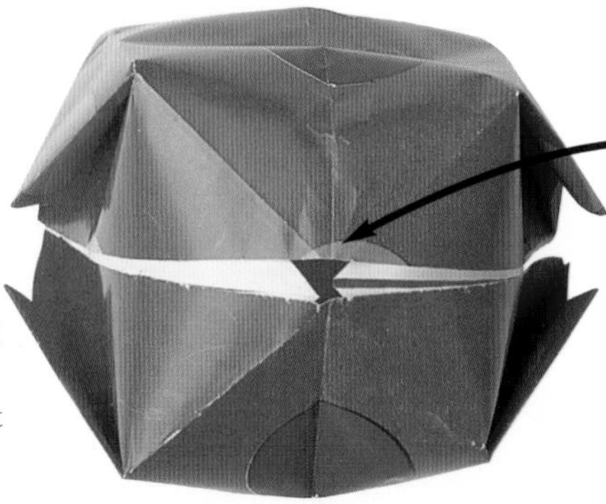

6 Now hold the shape gently and blow into the hole at the top.

Blow

It should puff out nicely. Now fill it with water through the hole and throw it!

Races

Think you're fast? Set up some races see if you can beat your friends. Star with simple running races, then try races, where you form teams, and as person in the team finishes, they tou the next person, who starts running.

44

Games with paper, games with balls, games with water, fun in the sun.

Drink on the go....

No cup handy? Here's a quick way to make one out of a piece of square paper.

1 Fold a square piece of paper in half to make a triangle shape.

2 Fold the corner of the triangle up as shown here.

3 Repeat with the other corner.

4 Fold down the top. Turn over and repeat on the other side.

Slurp!

Shadow tag

Instead of touching each other, as in a game of tag, try jumping on each other's shadow. The person chasing tries to stand on someone's shadow; when they do that person becomes the chaser. You won't find it easy!

You can't catch me!

Here, catch the ball

Obstacle course

Ask an adult for some bits and pieces from around the yard or house that you can use to set up an obstacle course. Then time each other to finish it.

Jump over the broom, hop on one leg through the tires, and kick the ball!

Soccer skills

The backyard is the best place to brush up on your soccer skills—you are less likely to cause damage! How many times can you keep the ball up using your knees?

Ready, set, GO! Get out in the sunshine—play some games,

Blowing bubbles

Make your own bubble mixture, then search your house for things that you think you could blow bubbles through. You can make lots and lots of tiny bubbles or great big ones.

Gently **blow** through the gaps.

Bubble recipe
Use 1 large cup of dishwashing liquid, then mix in two large pitchers of water.

Mix the recipe in a big bowl

what makes a good bubble?

Bend wire or old coathangers into shapes to make you own blowers.

Boing

water squirters

One of the most refreshing ways to cool off in the hot sun is to get completely soaked. So put on your swimsuit, and if you don't have a water squirter, then try making one. Plastic bottles are good, but try old shampoo or dishwashing liquid bottles too. It's all a matter of experimenting.

Ball games

Any ball games are fun. If you have a lot of friends with you, then split into teams and compete against each other. Choose a team captain and make sure you agree on the rules before you start. If you want to play soccer, set up goal posts using bits and pieces found around your backyard.

Hide and seek

Ask a friend to count to 50 and find the best hiding place you can in the backyard. Stay very still and very quiet and wait until the seeker finds you. The first to be found is the seeker the next time. Sometimes the best hiding places are the most obvious ones. Remember, hold still!

★ **Ask an adult** to watch you when you are around water.

Here, catch the ball

… and hideaways

A secret camp in the backyard is a great way to keep out of the sun and to form a club. Decide who is going to be in your club and give it a name. You could even give homemade badges to members. Choose a password and only allow members to enter.

47

INDEX

ACKNOWLEDGMENTS

With thanks to the models . . .
Eleanor Bates, Luke Bower,
Charlotte, Billy and James Bull,
Seriye Ezigwe, Max, Guy and Imogen
Lowrie for being little rays of sunshine

The publishers would like to thank the
following for their kind permission to
reproduce their photographs:
(Abbreviations key: t=top, b=bottom,
r=right, c=center)

43tl Stuart McClymont, 43tr Corbis:
Richard Ransier;, 43bl Getty Images: Robert
Stahl; 44r Corbis: Peter N. Fox; 45c Getty
Images: Robert Stahl; 46r Corbis: Peter
Steiner; 47l Corbis: Dirk Douglass.

All other images © Dorling Kindersley.
For further information see:
www.dkimages.com